The Revolutionary Social Worker

Love Ethic Companion

Dyann Ross

IIR

REVOLUTIONARIES

Brisbane, Australia

ISBN 978-0-6487999-0-0

Cover artwork by Amanda Espinosa
Book design and typesetting by Paula Pomer

First published in 2020

Revolutionaries
Brisbane, Australia
www.revolutionaries.com.au

Acknowledgements

I wish to acknowledge the Gubbi Gubbi People of the Sunshine Coast area and pay my respects to them for their stewardship of this land and for their wisdom and ongoing contribution to Australian society.

I also wish to acknowledge people who seek to learn about nonviolence, love and ecojustice to live loving and peaceful lives. I am grateful for the opportunity to teach and learn with each new generation of social work students who will become the next ambassadors of revolutionary love.

I am grateful to the director of Revolutionaries for creating a book company dedicated to love as revolutionary ways of being in the world.

Contents

Introduction

Hello to you dear Reader,

Thank you for picking up my book. As the first step, let me introduce myself to you.

I am sitting at my desk on a very rainy day in early autumn and pondering how to share my ideas with you. Outside my window I can see the enormous trunks and branches of several mango trees that are over 100 years old. These magnificent trees are home to bats, kookaburras, parrots, snakes, crows, doves, and other winged and slithering creatures. One of our four-legged family members, Frankie, is lying on the mat beside my chair. Frankie is the cutest Australian terrier now getting on in years. Her buddy is a rambunctious wolf-hound-cross-something, Winnie, who is edgy today because the rain stopped us having their early morning walk. We live in a rambling Queenslander house on a treed hill in a little town just north of Brisbane, and from our front verandah we see the beautiful Mt Ninderry.

I've made this set of ethics resources its very own little book so it is easy to carry around and also affordable to buy. It is a companion to *The Revolutionary Social Worker: The Love Ethic Model* book based on hooks' (2000) love ethic. A student introduced me to bell hooks' books way back, and her writing has continued to inspire me ever since. Do you know her work? Shout out to the student for this life changing gift.

My big dilemma has been how to offer this book while not presuming to know what you do not know or should know. I know you will have your own ideas and cherished values and perhaps are already working in your chosen profession. Feel free to treat it as a smorgasbord of materials and help yourself to anything that you wish to include in your practice model.

The logic, if I can claim to be logical about a passionate writing project, guiding the material is my learning from many years as a social worker. If I had this material at the beginning of my career or really any time during it, I believe it would have been most helpful. Is it strange to be passionate about ethics and ethical theories? Probably!

While I was preparing this book, I kept students in my Ethics courses in mind. My hope is that it is a useful resource for students, practitioners and anyone interested in refreshing, or building for the first time, their ethical literacy. Ethical literacy is living and practising with heart language.

Bye for now,

Dyann

Love ethic informed resources

The book is a companion resource for *The Revolutionary Social Worker: The Love Ethic Model* which outlines values and ethics for loving, anti-oppressive practice. It shares the same lead title to denote its relevance for revolutionary social work practice. While it is a stand-alone resource, it is best read in conjunction with the first book. The companion resource provides a love ethic informed interpretation of ethical theories and ethico-legal principles. These theories and principles underpin the revolutionary social worker's ability to practice according to the love ethic model. I recommend an additional seven new ethico-legal principles as suggested by the love ethic for revolutionary practice. Examples of the international conventions and declarations as well as Australian legislation and statements are provided, which can guide contributions to upholding the public interest. The public interest is the highest expression of the ethics of love, nonviolence and ecojustice where there are movements towards these ethics in specific situations.

It is the case that all theories and legislation have at least implicit ethical dimensions. The book focuses on theories that are explicit in their ethical premises and shows the key assumptions, claims, practice strategies and limitations of each theory. Theory limitations are used as pivot points to show how a reflexive stance (Fook, 2016) that is love ethic informed can guide the practitioner in the use of the theories without being ethically compromised. This necessarily involves an 'in situ' ability to act with power-sensitive and context-sensitive skills to apply the ethical ideas.

Personal and professional values are the building blocks of ethical practice. Theories are sophisticated statements about values and principles. The revolutionary social worker fosters professional integrity in all their actions. To achieve this they need to be skilled in aligning their values with relevant theories to guide their practice. It is really important that you reflect upon your actions and understand what is influencing you to act as you do. The point of being reflective is to then be willing to change or adjust your actions to be congruent with your values (Miehls & Moffatt, 2000). If your values have been compromised, the first step is to understand why to ensure you are working non-reactively with any harmful power dynamics involved. Realising the rights and wellbeing of a person, animal or ecosystem could depend on your reflective and self-adjusting capacities. Additionally, this self-reflective work needs to be paralleled with a critical and loving understanding of the contextual and political influences on your practice. The outcome of this parallel contextualised reflective thinking can be a more nuanced, strategic, and if necessary, resistive response.

While social workers tend to have an aversion to claiming expertise, professional integrity hinges on competent and accountable professional practice. There is a complexity of considerations regarding what counts as competence and accountability, and in the latter instance, to whom the practitioner is accountable. Accountability is a key dimension of professional integrity and refers to the use of professional authority to uphold ethical responsibilities. This can be experienced as divided loyalties that the practitioner needs to navigate, where workplaces will have strong norms that typically reinforce the status quo of power relations. These norms may be in tension with the agency's professed mission of service to people who access the agency. Further, loyalty to service users can be in tension with loyalty to work colleagues, managers and the profession (Australian Association of Social Workers [AASW], 2010, p. 4). An implication of the love ethic is that practitioners are to be accountable to the least powerful individual or group in any particular situation (Ross, 2017).

An aspect of ethical practice involves recognising other peoples' values and ethics may be different and possibly even incompatible or in conflict with your own (Hugman, 2013). The idea of ethical pluralism tries to grapple with this complexity by acknowledging that "there may be plausible cultural differences in values" (Hugman, 2013, p. 76), including how values are interpreted and enacted. There may also be pressing power differences intersecting with cultural factors, such as elite groups' political and economic agendas (Woodley, 2020). These power differences can skew whose values are to be upheld and whose may be denied. Thus, ethical pluralism, if interpreted as 'all ethics are equally good and valid,' can hide the ethical undesirability of violence, lovelessness and eco-injustice.

The love ethic model is premised on a willingness to recognise and respect all parties' ethics in a contested situation. This is provided the consequences of those ethics do not harm or compromise the rights and interests of others (including nonhuman others). As a result, ethical pluralism and the related idea of ethical relativism need to be subjected to context-sensitive and power-sensitive analysis of the specific ethics involved. In turn, ethical absolutism is the other end of the continuum where there are certain ethical principles which are not tolerated. In situations of violence and injustice, the revolutionary social worker may, at the very least, have to resort to nonviolent direct actions, non co-operation and appeals to legal sanctions. Love ethic work involves challenging, resisting and changing the causes of violence, lovelessness and eco-injustice. Here the inextricable link between power and ethics is evident, and in turn, this is the main focus of love ethic work.

The contexts of practice are so complex that no one ethical theory will be sufficient to guide you in how to influence and challenge the status quo to achieve loving, anti-oppressive goals. The adoption of a love ethic informed interpretation of ethical theories and principles will assist the revolutionary social worker in utilising all the theories with some cautions and refinements. It can be discouraging that the efficacy of love ethic oriented theories are not appreciated due to the difficulty of achieving anti-oppressive goals. This view is yet another opportunity to resist what Freire (1970) calls fatalism, where the status quo is accepted due to the belief that something better is not possible.

When considering the material in the book, you are invited to filter its usefulness through your own ethical positionality and through a loving critique of your profession. For example, in the 2010 version of the *Code of Ethics*, the AASW have watered down an earlier statement supporting a professional obligation to resist unfair laws and policies. It explains that:

> Tensions may occasionally arise between observing the Code and complying with legal organisational requirements. (AASW, 2020, p. 14)

Given social work's social justice mission, it could be expected that this would be followed with imploring the practitioner to resist and stand with the oppressed if those requirements are unfair. Instead the statement continues:

Social workers must act in accordance with the law and with organisational directives. (2020, p. 14)

There is an implicit subtext that laws and directives are fair and ethical. The opportunity to promote an informed activism is side-stepped with the concluding point:

If the law or organisational directives conflict with perceived moral obligations, a social worker should seek guidance from a senior colleague. (AASW, 2010, p. 14)

Individualist and professionally sanitised notions of ethical practice and accountability need unsettling and augmenting with power-sensitive communitarian ethics (McAuliffe, 2014). Further, a critical understanding is needed of how dominant ideas and people are located at the top of power hierarchies with a range of mechanisms of power to avoid accountability (Mullaly & West, 2017).

The beliefs and ideas that can support love ethic work are now considered by describing ethical theories and refining them with a loving, anti-oppressive framing and interpretation. This is followed by an outline of ethico-legal principles and their re-interpretation to be consistent with the love ethic. The love ethic implies several additional ethico-legal principles, such as anti-discrimination and the precautionary principle, are required. The companion resource concludes with a selection of the international conventions, declarations, (Australian) legislation and public statements which can guide the upholding of the interests, rights and wellbeing of people, animals and the environment.

Synopsis of ethical theories

Hello again dear Reader,

It is a new day and I'm back at my desk. Last night there was a commotion in the chook pen, and we rushed down with our trusty brooms in hand to find a python snake in with the chooks. Needless to say it was a very stressful situation and while the chooks survived, the snake went off under the house still hungry.

Here we are with the theories. Not everyone's idea of fun, but they can be very useful in professional practice. Acting on hunches or repeating what you did last time can be hard to justify if something doesn't go too well.

In this section, I provide you with some detailed accounts of a range of ethical theories. It is interesting to me that I've started with the two dominant theories. Deontology and consequentialism have been so influential in Western thinking and governance of nation states, including my own home country, Australia. Bear with me as starting in this way allows me to build towards the love ethic theory and why it is needed. The love ethic theory, which includes the Eastern philosophy of Taoism, is my integration of the best of all the other ethical theories. I package them for ready use by the revolutionary social worker-cum-citizen, which is you, dear reader.

Suffice it to say, the order of presentation of the ethical theories is not in order of how much I've been influenced by them, or inclusive of all the influences on my practice. I thought it may be useful to organise the outlines of the ethical theories according to assumptions, claims, practice strategies, limitations and a love ethic informed guide. The aim is to show you these building blocks of each theory in the hope it makes the theories easy to understand and easy to take ideas and use them. I don't usually think in such a structured way about theories. I tend to cherry-pick ideas from all sorts of places if they seem interesting. Are you ready? Let's jump into it.

Deontology or duty-based

Source: Kant, in McAuliffe (2014); Pullen-Sansfacon & Cowden (2012); Beckett, Maynard & Jordan (2017)

Deontology assumptions (key beliefs)

Individuals are rational beings

Individuals are moral beings

Individuals should accept the rule of law

The rule of law represents societal good

There is a right response

This right response is clear

Ethics are absolutist – there is no need to consider different views and values

Knowledge as objective facts.

Deontology claims

Individuals are valued in their own right and not as means to an end

Based on the concept of inalienable human rights

Obligation to rules, laws and agency policies

Some principles sit above others

The course of action is clear and absolute

Right action is more important than good outcomes

The exercise of power is legitimated by implementing the right response

Individual autonomy is valued above responsibility to others

Service user self-determination, respect and acceptance are to be upheld

Justice as individual rights e.g., to privacy and freedom of association.

Deontology practice strategies & implications

Always relate to individuals with respect and support their self-determination

Uphold the best intention of legislation and policies

Uphold agency procedures and workplace instructions for the good of service users

Be well informed about the agency's legal, administrative policies and procedures

Follow and comply with the agency's rules and requirements

Well-founded rules are important for consistency and accountability in practice

Seek legal and professional advice if an individual's rights are transgressed.

Deontology limitations

Presumes society can be made equal and fair through legislation and rules

The laws and rules may not be fair for some individuals

The right response is not necessarily clear or uncontested

Presumes human service organisations are benevolent providers of services

Onus is on service user to understand the system to make complaints without being disadvantaged

Reinforces dominance of rationality and reason

Can reinforce dominant power groups' views as truth

Human-centric bias not addressed

Duty to one individual may conflict with duty to another individual

May have conflicting duties towards an individual, e.g., where their right to freedom conflicts with their right to protection

If someone isn't considered rational (capable of rational thought), should they be treated as without intrinsic worth?

May be conflicting obligations that are not recognised or that are compromised

Emotional literacy and a caring regard less valued as rationality is the key value

The theory is a-contextual, a-cultural and a-political

Minority groups or individuals may be silenced or sacrificed by the practitioner upholding the law.

Love ethic informed guide for deontology

Some love ethic informed ideas and practice implications include:

Extend ethical sphere of concern to nonhuman animals and the environment

Validate emotional, embodied and other ways of knowing, communicating, and reasoning

Affirm collective rights and interests alongside individual rights and interests

Use professional discernment in the interpretation of laws and policies

Resist and challenge unfair agency rules and requirements

Lobby for legislation changes to unfair laws

Provide worker education on interpreting legislation and policy to uphold individual rights of service users

Ensure service users are informed of their rights and give consent for any interventions

Enable individuals to access legal advice if rights are threatened

Support own profession's lobbying and advocacy work

Undertake ongoing self-education to maximise own competencies and knowledge

Research new innovations and service user-led experiences and initiatives

Support minority group activism

Document failures of the agency to uphold the rights and interests of service users

Provide well documented evidence of discrimination to internal reviews, external accreditation and public inquiries.

Consequentialism, also called utilitarianism

Source: Mill, in McAuliffe (2014); Mill, Rawls, in Pullen-Sansfacon & Cowden (2012)

Consequentialism assumptions (key beliefs)

Many of the assumptions as deontology ethical theory, and additionally:

Ability of humans to feel joy and pain entitles them to moral status

People are rational beings

The rule of law represents societal good

The good is reflected in the majority view or action

Morality is located in the consequences of decisions and actions.

Consequentialism claims:

The right thing to do is that which maximises the good

Good outcomes are more important than how the outcome is achieved

Greatest good for the greatest number should be pursued

Weigh up the pros and cons of actions in terms of outcomes

General welfare of people valued rather than the individual's rights

Question asked is 'What would serve the greatest good?'

Justice as equal opportunity and equal distribution of resources (Rawls, 1971).

Consequentialism practice strategies & implications

Many of the practice strategies noted for deontology theory, and:

All actions can and should be considered in terms of their likely outcome and benefit for all involved

The goal of ethical practitioners is to have positive effects and outcomes

Develop and apply a public interest test

For example, in the *Right to Information Act 2009* it relates to whether to release information being requested:

> To determine the balance of the public interest, you must follow the process:
>
> 1. Identify any irrelevant factors and disregard them
>
> 2. Identify any relevant public interest factors favouring disclosure and nondisclosure
>
> 3. Balance the relevant factors favouring disclosure and nondisclosure; and

4. Decide whether disclosure of the information would, on balance, be contrary to the public interest. (Queensland Government, 2009, n.p.)

Consequentialism limitations

Many of the limitations relevant to deontology theory, and:

Minority groups or members may be silenced or sacrificed for the majority

Powerful individuals and groups can unfairly influence what is the public good

The public good will be contested and not necessarily clear

The public interest test, therefore, can be biased to serve political interests

Presumes the public will support promised outcomes with no regard for minority groups and the environment

The consequences for whom?— The individual carrying out the action? Everyone except the individual carrying out the action? Everyone?

How can the individual know what will lead to the greatest good?

What is meant by good?

Is morality to be determined by the majority view of the greatest good?

If not, how is it to be determined?

Some actions, even though they might lead to good for a great number of people, are intolerable (e.g., using a child for painful and fatal medical experimentation even if it could lead to saving other childrens' lives)

Should the needs of some people be counted (or weighted) differently to the needs of others?

Love ethic informed guide for consequentialism

Some love ethic informed ideas and practice implications include:

Adopt Fraser's (2009) notion of justice as a dialogical process between individuals of equal moral value

The decision about what constitutes positive effects and outcomes needs to include the individual in a partnership with the practitioner

Consideration of the likely benefits for all cannot only be a decision made by the high power individual or group

The public interest test needs to be applied in a transparent, inclusive and democratic process

Harm that occurs to low power individuals and minority groups is to be recognised

Fair compensation and redress for adversely impacted parties is required.

While deontology and consequentialism are recognised as two different ethical theories, they have much in common and can be used in an anti-oppressive way if the love ethic informed guide is followed. Further, the revolutionary social worker will often draw on aspects of these theories in tandem with relevant aspects of all the ethical theories included in the book. It is to be cautioned, though, that these two theories tend towards reinforcing the status quo if over-relied upon to the exclusion of caring and anti-oppressive ethical influences.

Virtues (qualities of character)

Source: Banks (2012, 2016); Banks & Gallagher (2009); Aristotle, McIntyre, in Pullen-Sansfacon & Cowden (2012)

Virtues theory assumptions (key beliefs)

Individuals are relational beings

Individuals are interdependent and influenced by others

Reality is socially constructed by individuals

Ethics is a social practice between individuals

Individuals will seek to be virtuous

Ethics are relativist, that is, it is important to consider the view of others

Individuals will seek the good life

Justice is achieved through virtuous actions of individuals.

Virtues theory claims

Emphasis is on the inherent qualities of the individual. That is, the emphasis is on the type of individual

Being of good character is measured by how the individual acts

Ethics conveyed through qualities of character, e.g., honesty, fairness and compassion

Acting virtuously is the way to the good life

A virtue is a highly developed capacity to act ethically. Thus, it tends to involve a combination of virtues

It also involves conscious decisions about which virtues to utilise for good in a situation

Virtues can be expressed as lack of and excess, e.g., the virtue of compassion, as a lack is indifference and as an excess is excessive concern (Pullen-Sansfacon & Cowden, 2012)

Motivated by values more than rules and duty

Not anti-rules or anti-duty, but does not unquestioningly follow rules

May act wrongly out of virtue, e.g., withhold truth to protect someone from being distressed

Acknowledges the other individual's virtues

Principle-based theories are not sufficient in deciding between right and wrong.

Virtues theory practice strategies & implications

The individual is expected to be self-aware and with this self-awareness, act for the good in the situation, utilising their personal skills and qualities

The question asked is - 'Are the actions what a virtuous individual would do?'

It is less clear what happens next if the answer is contested or their action causes harm

The focus may need to be on assisting and encouraging the individual to act with desirable traits, such as open-mindedness and compassion, and to couple this with the virtue of critical reflection regarding their use of power

Public, professional and workplace education (without coercion) is important to foster virtuous citizens

Risks to public or personal safety may over-ride respect for the service user and their ability to act in a virtuous way

Adopting strengths-based approaches (Saleebey, 2012) in practice can support the individual to be virtuous

Utilising interpersonal skills and processes is presumed to be a virtue for the practitioner

Obtaining professional supervision would also be considered a virtue (assuming the individual is willing to be self-reflective and change their behaviour if needed)

Empathy and person-centred approaches (Rogers, 1951/2003) can validate the individual's virtues.

Virtues theory limitations

May draw upon deontology and consequentialist theories and therefore the noted limitations for these theories need to be addressed

Can risk constructing virtues, and the lack of virtues, as fixed and given personality traits

An individual can act virtuously but still not experience the good life

What constitutes virtuous behaviour (and the good life) is culturally and context sensitive. Thus, it is not self-evident or universally agreed what a virtue is in any given situation

Power is entwined with virtues and can be used to justify harmful and unjust actions

This can collude with essentialist, biological arguments which are the basis for discrimination

Human-centric bias means the virtues of nonhuman animals and nature are not recognised

An unequal relationship between practitioner and service user may undermine the valuing of the service user's virtues and strengths

Practitioner's use of authority e.g., duty of care, may undermine individual's self-efficacy and ability to act virtuously to empower themselves, e.g., when resisting forced mental health treatment is interpreted as non-compliance

A practitioner can be virtuous in their own view and that of their employer, and may nevertheless cause offence, harm and injustice

The types of virtues needing to be expressed in a specific situation may be unclear or contested

Virtues as a possession of an individual may not equate with actions that contribute to an individual's wellbeing, safety and justice

Justice requires virtues, but good people who strive to be virtuous is not a sufficient condition to ensure justice is achieved. Virtuous people are necessary though for revolutionary work.

Love ethic informed guide for virtues theory

Strengths-based ideas (Saleebey, 2012) have made an important contribution to the implementation of virtues ethical theory in inter-personal and community social work practice. Virtues theory can be integral to care-based approaches and adapted to be compatible with anti-oppressive, First Nation Peoples' world views and posthumanist theories and practices. Virtues ethics using the strengths approach can also be embedded in deontology and consequentialist theories to assist in tempering the focus on rational rule following. It may need augmenting with anti-oppressive ethics to avoid colluding with harm caused by dominant individuals and authoritarian organisations.

A love ethic informed guide to virtues ethical theory would aim to address the limitations that may be relevant in any specific relationship or situation. See the claims and practice implications in all the following ethical theories.

Care-based (care and relationship)

Source: Banks (2012, 2016); Pease, Vreugdenhil & Stanford (2018); Tong, 1988; Pullen-Sansfacon & Cowden (2012)

Care-based theory assumptions (key beliefs)

All of the virtue theory assumptions, and:

Moral capacity can be learned

Ethics is about how individuals act, not abstract principles

Reality is subjective, not purely objective

An individual can be ethical if they are caring

Emotions are a form of knowledge

Caring about others is integral to ethics

Justice occurs through and in relationships.

Care-based theory claims

Emotions, not only rationality, as the basis for morality

Further, emotional responsiveness and mutual interdependence is valued

Emphasises qualities required to help other people (and thus interlinks with virtues theory)

Focuses on the relationship with the individual

Values connection, caring and trust

Actions judged as they impact on and appeal to relationship

Also emphasises taking responsibility in relationships

Ethics is practical and expressed 'in situ' with others

Emphasises responsibility rather than duty; relationships rather than principles

Supports commitment to dialogical (equal) relations between practitioners and service users

With its emphasis on relationship, compassion and nurturing, the theory provides an important resource for challenging managerialist and technocratic approaches to human service provision.

Care-based theory practice strategies & implications

Includes the practice strategies relevant to virtues theory and, additionally:

The question asked is – 'What does a caring response require in this situation?' (McAuliffe, 2014)

Thus, lead with expressing caring regard and respect for the individual

Fostering a caring, respectful relationship occurs simultaneously with responding to the individual's concerns

Caring does not obviate the need to hold the individual accountable for their actions

Nor does it obviate the practitioner's responsibility to the individual and others in their life

Relevant principles may be overlooked, e.g., duty to warn

Includes a commitment to all involved, not only individual autonomy and rights at any cost

Listen for the contextual and cultural influences that are conveyed in the individual's experiences

Seek ways to address the impacts on the individual's wellbeing

This ideally involves fostering an equal relationship with service users

Thus, strategies such as co-partnering and co-design models of service delivery and service user peer workforce could be fostered as part of power sharing in the professional relationship (Happell & Scholz, 2017).

Care-based theory limitations

Tends to focus on individual responsibility and relationships, neglecting a collective responsibility for lack of care for minority groups

May neglect invisible structural relationships of power which are embedded in social policies, organisational regulations and legislation

Care can occur in tandem with controlling and oppressive practices

At the same time, if legal coercion is involved, this heightens the need for care and respect towards the individual

A care focus can result in actions to create safety which may be experienced as coercive by the individual

Care-based ethics may place too much emphasis on individual relationships rather than overall principles

Can over-invest in emotional support at the expense of addressing power issues in relationships

Baltra-Ulloa (2018) explains that colonialist notions of care and caring remain embedded in Western culture and politics, which is based on hierarchical and thus unequal relationships

Therefore, there is a need to avoid universal definitions and claims [for the practitioner] to be able to hear individuals "speak about themselves while they formulate what care is in their language" (Baltra-Ulloa, 2018, p. 137).

Human-centric bias and privilege not addressed

Practitioners experiencing a lack of care in their workplace need to be supported

Justice involves caring as a necessary aspect of justice work, but it is not sufficient to ensure justice is achieved.

Love ethic informed guide for care-based theory

Perhaps the most troubling aspect of care-based ethics is how the language of care, can belie acts of harm and lack of love (Hughes, 2018). It is important that any misalignment between language and actions is 'called out'. Just as violence in a relationship, even if love is proclaimed, means this is not a loving relationship, so too with claims of care in relationships. The critique is not exclusive to care-based ethics as harm can occur without any care being seen as needed or a duty of care being seen to exist. For example, consequentialism gives ethical credence to Australia's *Border Protection Act 2015*, which results in asylum seekers being intercepted at sea and taken to an offshore detention centre. In the name of the greatest good for Australia's security, the internationally recognised human rights of the asylum seekers to seek asylum are waived. According to Barns & Newhouse, the Act "effectively turns the Department of Immigration into a secret security organisation with police powers" (2015, n.p.). This is compounded by its censure of concerned individuals speaking out about harm. Silence in situations of violence and harm is very dangerous to the moral fibre of a society. Unfair legislation cannot be allowed to be implemented without being resisted and in this sense, care can guide ethical practice. Doctors for Refugees challenged this part of the legislation by arguing their right to undertake medical advocacy in the High Court (Doherty, 2016). As a result, the Australian Government conceded some professionals' right to make public statements, but social work is one profession that can still incur two years jail time for unauthorised disclosures (Doherty, 2016).

Anti-oppressive and feminist

Source: Clifford & Burke (2009); hooks (2000); Smith (1990); Hill Collins (1990); Stanley & Wise (1983); Haraway (2006); Doyle (2016, 2019)

Anti-oppressive and feminist assumptions (key beliefs)

This diverse grouping of ethical theories builds upon virtues and care-based ideas and extends them while unsettling certainty claims and accenting power inequalities. The assumptions are similar and additionally include:

Reality is not given, final, or monolithic

Individuals tend to act as if it were fixed, and how things are is thus thought to be inevitable

Individual experiences, if validated, can unsettle this fatalism

Individual actions occur in a social context

Social context is more than the individual's actions

Care and other virtues involve the exercise of power in relationships

Ethics and power are interconnected and not separable

An unequal society is perpetuated by inequality in relationships, both direct and indirect

It is unethical to use power to cause or reinforce oppression

Collective freedom and welfare are emphasised, especially of minority groups

Care of people and critical understanding of oppression underpins justice work to address inequality.

Anti-oppressive and feminist claims

Individual virtues may not be sufficient to enable ethical practice

The individual's experience, including emotions, is central to feminist practice

Different individuals experience oppression differently, even if part of the same minority group

The individual can internalise oppression and blame themselves

The social context is unequal, and this can cause harm and compound disadvantage

People oppress people, not institutions and structures (Stanley & Wise, 1983)

Lack of care and lovelessness towards others and self-serving virtues can reinforce inequality

27

Privilege, extreme wealth and authoritarian power can disadvantage minority groups

Domination of women (and children) by men is the main concern of feminism

Sexual oppression is closely related to other types of violence, e.g., domestic violence, against women and other minority status groups

Pease, Vreugdenhil & Stanford's ideas can be paraphrased as:

Care and care-giving are influenced by the social, cultural and political context

Care and care-giving are thus influenced by the intersectionality of oppression, e.g., gender, race, class, location and employment

Caring in an unequal society can reinforce injustice, such as gender bias in caring roles (2018, pp. 7-8).

Justice work is a societal responsibility, not an individual's responsibility solely or mainly

It is not the responsibility of the uncared for and unjustly treated to address inequality

The status quo will continue unless challenged and resisted

Justice work is motivated by caring for people and can reflect similar intersectional bias against the individual, e.g., unpaid activism by minority groups

Bodily autonomy and self-determination can be threatened by coercion and violence

Caring in professional relationships can be used to control minority groups

Human service organisations can recreate oppressive relationships, in the name of care

To summarise, according to McDonald & Then, three key feminist ideas are:

> Oppression of certain social groups exists e.g., women, ethnic minorities, people with a disability; this oppression may be experienced differently by members of each group, but it is a moral

and political wrong; and, oppression needs to be addressed at its source in societal norms, discourses, and institutions. (2014, p. 6)

Anti-oppressive and feminist practice strategies & implications

The goal is individual and collective empowerment

Empowerment makes justice work possible and sustainable

Involves making the links between personal experiences and political context

Group-based strategies are key to bringing people with shared experiences together

Resisting and challenging inequalities and prejudices are the main skill sets needed

Justice is about upholding the rights and meeting the needs of people

Justice is also about the accountability of individuals or organisations who cause harm

Can draw on duty-based ideas, consequentialism and virtues, with caution regarding their limitations

Can also be enacted through a care-based approach

That is, care and justice both needed to address oppression

Anti-oppressive practice requires a reflective and self-correcting approach by the practitioner regarding their own use of power

Requires that the practitioner is aware of the organisational, political and other contextual influences on their practice

According to Clifford & Bourke, anti-oppressive ethics is about:

Taking thorough account of social difference

Evaluating the range and impact of social systems and relationships

Understanding the specific social histories of individuals and groups involved

Analysing different kinds of power, [and]

Examining own social location and exploring the possibility of dialogue. (2009, pp. 29-38)

Anti-oppressive ethics influences practice to avoid blaming the individual for issues beyond their immediate influence.

Anti-oppressive and feminist limitations

Human-centric focus. (Extended by eco-feminism to include animals and the environment)

Feminism is a set of influential anti-establishment theories and is blamed for causing social disharmony (hooks, 2000). This can make collectivising with an explicit anti-oppressive stance difficult and doing so can even risk backlash and violence

Need to be aware of the diversity of views within feminist theorising

Can exacerbate dualistic thinking between, for example, women-men; the oppressed-oppressor; the powerful-powerless; perpetrator-victim; enemy-ally

Feminism has been critiqued as white women's theory; however, feminism tends to now be inclusive of all types of oppression

This criticism should not be used as a smoke screen to discount or hide all the grassroots, people power justice work that has always been the defining feature of womens' liberation and other liberation movements

Any theory or organised stance against dominant groups in society will meet with backlash and discrediting of leaders

Much is expected and needed of anti-oppressive theories, and they can be found to be inadequate in challenging situations.

Love ethic informed guide for anti-oppressive and feminist theory

Anti-oppressive and feminist ethical theories are utilised in complex, contested and often very unequal situations of power. They are thereby subject to similar challenges as love ethic theory and other non dominant ideas that challenge the status quo and relations of ruling (Smith, 1990). Standpoint minority theories are not specifically acknowledged, but are an important influence in the loving, anti-oppressive ethical landscape, and include queer, trans and critical disability theories (for example, see Fuss, 1991; Butler, 1990; Bettcher, 2015). Resistance and refusal to accept inequality, all forms of discrimination and harm remain the baseline methods of nonviolent, anti-oppressive action that can enable practitioners to maintain some ethical integrity in repressive situations.

First Nation Peoples' world views

Source: Green (2018); Watson (1988); Bennett (2019); Smith (1999); Poelina (2020); Woodley (2020)

First Nation Peoples' world views assumptions (key beliefs)

There is an interconnectedness between people, animals and the environment (Green, 2018; Poelina, 2020)

All beings have equal intrinsic value and worth

The law is in the land not in the people (Poelina, 2020)

Mother Nature creates and sustains all of life

A human being is spiritual, emotional, physical and emotional, not only rational

Community and group are of higher value than the individual

Knowledge is created through a diversity of actors, across species and nature, and is more than a human capacity.

First Nation Peoples' world views claims

Humans are in relationship with all that is, a holistic ecological beingness

Racism is a pervasive prejudice against non dominant minority groups caused by white privilege

Individuals have obligations beyond their own interests and needs

Australian Aboriginal and Torres Strait Islander People have not ceded their rights, and as such they claim sovereignty as First Nation People

Non-indigenous people need to address historical and contemporary harmful impacts of colonisation, including attempts at genocide and the Stolen Generation (Bennett, 2019)

It is an offence under Bunya (lore) to not provide for others (Green, 2018)

Learn the laws of the land, from the land (Watson, 1988; Poelina, 2020)

All citizens need to take on the same responsibilities of stewardship as First Nation People (Watson, 1988; Woodley, 2020).

First Nation Peoples' world views practice strategies & implications

Practice "Dadirri - deep and respectful listening" (Mareese Terare cited in Funston, 2013)

Undertake decolonising work at the personal, organisational and societal levels to address systemic racism

Violence needs to be understood as a product of the socio-political context not a consequence of First Nation Peoples' cultures (Funston, 2013)

Avoid appropriating First Nations Peoples' knowledge, culture and lands

Practice cultural humility by being accountable to the people (Fisher-Borne, Cain & Martin, 2015)

Learn from First Nation People what they want to feel safe interacting with non-indigenous people

Support calls for sovereignty and treaty

Stand with First Nation People to provide stewardship of nature

Develop a group-based society where the relationship between people, and between people and the land, is non competitive (Watson,

1988)

As a consequence, individuals will neither aspire nor be allowed to become rich and powerful at the expense of the land or of other people (Watson, 1988)

Address how Indigenous knowledge is obtained and valued, for example, according to Smith, research ethics with Maori People should:

Show respect for people

Present yourself to the people face to face

Look, listen […] speak (in that order)

Share and host people - be generous

Be cautious

Do not trample over the mana of people

Do not flaunt your knowledge. (1999, p. 120)

First Nation Peoples' world views limitations

It is not the prerogative of a non-indigenous writer to provide a list of limitations of First Nation Peoples' world views.

The limitations tend to cohere around the failure of dominant groups, including social work (Bennett, 2019), in Australian society to move past the symbolism of the national apology in 2008. The moral imperative was to build on the apology to substantially redress the harm caused by colonialism and ongoing racism. The failure of the Closing the Gap national level initiative to address key indicators of racism is a case in point. Oscar and Little (2019) explain that in fact the gap has widened since its inception in 2008.

Love ethic informed guide for First Nation Peoples' world views

The love ethic informed guide acknowledges the diversity, and within that diversity, the holistic, caring and non exploitative ways of First Nation Peoples' world views. Non-indigenous revolutionary social workers stand with the ongoing efforts of First Nation People to gain sovereignty and integral to that, land rights and social justice. Further, they dedicate to their own and others' decolonising work to address personal and systemic racism.

The differences between the ethical theories in this collection can be discerned by referring to specific authors.

Posthumanist, ecofeminist, and pro-animal

Source: Plumwood (1993, 2000, 2002); Shiva & Mies (2014); Haraway (2006, 2010, 2017); Boetto (2019); Braidotti (2013, 2018); Francione & Charlton (2013); Singer (2015); White (2018)

Posthumanist, ecofeminist and pro-animal assumptions (key beliefs)

Compatible with all the assumptions of First Nation Peoples' world views, with particular emphasis on:

The interconnection between humans, nonhuman animals and the environment

Humans are part of nature

Humans do not own or have an inalienable right to use animals and exploit nature

The agency and equal moral worth of all species and nature

Cultural diversity and species diversity need to be honoured and protected

Equal consideration of species' interests

Human consciousness is not a premise for devaluing animals and nature

Nonhuman animals experience enjoyment and pain

Human privilege needs to be challenged

Purist animal ethics believe animals are not to be abused and killed for human consumption

Justice is holistic and inclusive of the rights of all sentient beings and nature

Further, justice equates with social, economic and environmental sustainability and flourishing.

Posthumanist, ecofeminist and pro-animal claims

Self-serving privilege such as extreme wealth and power by society's power elites causes harm, loss and injustice

There are social patterns of discrimination against minority groups

Discrimination is against people who are constructed as less valued than their desirable 'other' and includes sexism, racism, homophobia, disablism, classism, geographical location and ageism

Minority groups comprise members who have at least one devalued social characteristic or identity

They may also experience an intersectionality of devalued identities

Minority group membership, while diverse, can be homogenised and devalued

This occurs by stigma and dominant discourses, which tend to blame individuals for their oppression

Individuals can experience oppression without identifying with a minority group

Minority groups can be targeted and repressed for seeking their rights and wellbeing

Laws can be unfair and reinforce discrimination and harm

Minority groups are resistive and actively challenge their oppression

Anthropocentrism (human-centred bias) has created an unsustainable planetary situation

Species extinction rates, climate change and deforestation are examples of unsustainability

Inequality between humans, especially sexism, manifests as devaluing of nonhuman animals and nature

Speciesism (bias against nonhuman animals), especially animals with an economic value, causes loss of freedom, harm and death

All sentient beings experience the world and as such can feel pain, and therefore are moral beings

Trees and other natural entities and non-sentient beings are part of the planetary life force

It is a state crime to allow the destruction of the environment and to not afford protection to beings and entities affected by this destruction.

Posthumanist, ecofeminist and pro-animal practice strategies & implications

Uphold a belief in the intrinsic value of all sentient beings and non-sentient entities

Recognise the implications of human dominance and claims of exceptionalism

Develop a holistic practice approach that includes human, animal and ecosystem justice strategies

Practice nonviolence towards animals and veganism

Promote animal rights and wellbeing

Care for and honour nonhuman animals and non-animal beings such as trees, rivers and mountains

Support international sustainable development goals

Understand the harmful and unsustainable impacts of developmentalism (unchecked capitalism)

Be aware of protests by low power, minority groups and stand with them

Ryan provides an outline of an animal inclusive code of ethics for social work, for example:

Value: Service to human and nonhuman individuals

The social work discipline holds service in the interests of human and nonhuman wellbeing, and social and species justice, as primary objectives. The fundamental goals of social work service are to:

Attend to the interests and needs of human and nonhuman individuals; and,

Enable human and nonhuman individuals to flourish. (2011, p. 169)

Align personal and professional values

Link being a professional with being a citizen to extend caring contribution beyond the workplace

Justice is actively caring for and enabling the voice of oppressed people, animals and the environment

Linked to this, justice involves efforts towards sustainability, the flourishing of all forms of life

And genuine reconciliation with, and sovereignty for, First Nation People.

Posthumanist, ecofeminist and pro-animal limitations

The limitations are similar to the limitations of anti-oppressive, feminist and First Nation Peoples' world views in so far as these are non dominant ideas of minority groups, their allies and advocates. Additionally:

Speciesism (discrimination against non-human beings) underpins anthropocentrism (human superiority) and justifies all other types of oppression (Lennard & Wolfe, 2017)

The ethical project of addressing speciesism is barely on the political agenda and has enormous implications for the nature of human societies

Thus, a limitation is the relative lack of public interest and pressure to challenge the use, abuse and killing of some species of animals which occurs on a massive scale each day

Individual resistance to harming animals is feasible and needs to collectivise to effect broader change

Climate change activism is broad spread internationally and beginning to receive national attention in Australia but arguably the changes needed are overdue and pressing

Governments have a vested interest in supporting polluting and environmentally degrading industries

As part of the power elite, governments only respond to public pressure when it is in their interests to do so

The limitation is thus not in terms of the ethical ideas per se, but in terms of the dominance of the power elites who are served by maintaining the status quo.

Love ethic informed guide for posthumanist, ecofeminist and pro-animal

The love ethic approach enfolds all these ethical ideas and integrates them with some refinements. The overall aim is to enable people power to be cultivated and sustained for the justice work for people, animals and the environment. The justice work is needed from the grassroots in communities and environments, to plush company board rooms and chambers of parliaments.

The differences between the ethical theories in this collection can be discerned by referring to specific authors.

Love ethic and Taoism

Source: hooks (2000, 2001); Godden (2017); Pease, Vreugdenhil & Stanford (2018); Ross (2017, 2020a, 2020b); Nhat Hahn (2001); Dalai Lama (1997); Lao Tzu (4th Century B.C.)

Love ethic and Taoism assumptions (key beliefs)

See virtues, care-based, anti-oppressive, First Nation Peoples' world views, feminist, ecofeminist, posthumanist and pro-animal ethical theories. Use with caution in regard to their respective limitations.

Additionally, the Eastern worldview of Taoism, which informs Confucianism and Buddhism, according to Lao Tzu includes:

Virtues of inner strength, discipline and integrity

Non-action - Wu Wei:

The Way is ever without action, yet nothing is left undone

Because the sage opposes no one, no one in the world would oppose them

Use justice to rule a country [...]. Use non-action to govern the world

Careful action:

Cautious, like crossing a river in the winter

The sage is sharp but does not cut, pointed but does not pierce, forthright but does not offend, bright but does not dazzle

Nature and world:

If Heaven and Earth are unable to persist, how could [the hu]man?

[The hu]man is ruled by Earth. Earth is ruled by Heaven. Heaven is ruled by the Way. The Way is ruled by itself

All things carry yin and embrace yang. They reach harmony by blending with the vital breath

Never take over the world to tamper with it. Those who want to tamper with it are not fit to take over the world

Opposites and paradoxes:

What is and what is not create each other

Misery is what happiness rests upon. Happiness is what misery lurks beneath

The highest virtue is not virtuous. Therefore, it has virtue. The lowest virtue holds on to virtue. Therefore, it has no virtue

Sometimes gain comes from losing, and sometimes loss comes from gaining. (4th Century BC)

Love ethic and Taoism claims

Love includes care as well as critical understanding, compassion and responsibility towards other people, animals and the environment

It also involves a willingness to learn and enable other individuals' learning to achieve loving, nonviolent and just relationships and situations

Love is part of the planetary life force (Buber, 1970)

Buber (1970) also regards love as a responsibility of an "I" for a "You"

Love is healing, transformatory, revolutionary (hooks, 2000; West, 2011)

Love is compassionate communication (Nhat Hahn, 2001)

Deepak Chopra writes:

> Love can heal
>
> Love can renew
>
> Love can make us safe
>
> Love can inspire us with its power
>
> Love can bring us closer to God. (1997, p. 3)

Individuals do not have to agree on the meaning of love to gain from experiencing it

A love ethic enfolds love, nonviolence and ecojustice as meta-ethics that support all other anti-oppressive ethics

Love enables movements from violence to nonviolence

Love enables movements from eco-injustice to ecojustice, in its many manifestations

Love is not violent, possessive, manipulative or controlling

If violence is present in a relationship, this is not love even if so called

Love is a high order ethical capacity, and thus, more than a feeling. Rather it is a conscious commitment to loving actions

According to van Stichel there is a dynamic inter-relationship between love and justice:

> Love offers motivation, the necessary attitude to get involved in advocacy for justice

Love understands that inequality marks the starting point of change efforts

Love opens up a contextual sensitivity, attentiveness, and responsivity so that one keeps seeing the concrete person behind the structures. (2014, p. 507)

Love ethic and Taoism practice strategies & implications

Practice nonviolent communication, see, for example Rosenberg (2009)

Seek movements in relationships and situations from-

Lovelessness, violence and eco-injustice

Towards-

Love, nonviolence and ecojustice

By enacting-

Love, nonviolence and ecojustice in the specificities of relationships, time, place and context.

This may require resisting, challenging and seeking to change the status quo

Practice with the skills, processes and ethical sensibilities of person-centred, strengths, narrative, empowerment, community and social development

Practice gentle, loving kindness in all aspects of life and work (Dalai Lama, 1997)

Provide education in nonviolence and nonviolent direct action for public campaigns against injustice

Develop transformational change leadership capacities and relationships (Ross & Palmer, 2020)

Practice self-love and self-healing (Chopra, 1997) to avoid vicarious trauma

Foster a community of like-minded and like-hearted people (Nhat Hahn, 1996)

Build and maintain personal and professional integrity (Lao Tzu, 4th Century B.C.)

The ethic of love approach draws together many ideas from other authors and accents-

Seeking social, species and environmental justice, with heart

With heart refers to practice and life wisdom, gentle loving kindness, respect, nonviolence and compassion

Taking responsibility for own actions, especially harm done, even if unintended

And enabling others to take responsibility for their own actions, again especially where harm is done, even if unintended

This needs to occur from a learning posture 'How can I do this differently?' not a posture of expecting and requiring the powerless parties to change or to hold the burden of cost and pain for the issue. As Bolton (1986) writes:

> There are three essentials for professional communication, genuineness, empathy and non-possessive love. Non-possessive love involves accepting, respecting, and the supporting of individuals [and animals] in a non-paternalistic and freeing way. (1986, p. 259)

The love ethic is about a willingness to act for one's own or others' learning in-situ and in power relations for the purpose of achieving the substantive aspects of justice relevant to the situation

Often this is about powerful people learning to take responsibility for the harmful effects of their behaviour (Ross, 2017).

Love ethic and Taoism limitations

Mullaly and West (2017) write that the powerful won't readily give up their/our privileges

Hence social justice needs to be struggled for nonviolently and with a love ethic as the moral compass

Struggles for justice are some of the most challenging actions whereby the more successful the campaigns, the higher the risk of backlash, including repression by the power elites. For example, the first gay and lesbian protesters in Australia in 1978 were imprisoned and abused. Many of them joined the 2020 celebration which saw 200 floats in the march including from mainstream organisations and sporting groups and tens of thousands of cheering public lining the route of the procession (see, https://www.mardigras.org.au/). As just one example, it is instructive of the risks that can go with the vision of equality and of the time it can take for public prejudices to shift from lovelessness or indifference to open-hearted love and celebration of sexual diversity

The challenge of maintaining hope of a better world and a belief in love as the way as well as the goal is a potential limitation in the face of daily media reports of violence, loss and degradation

The limitations are not in relation to the love ethic ideas per se but in the potential in specific relationships and situations to enable movements away from what hooks (1994) calls an ethic of domination.

Love ethic informed guide for love ethic and Taoism

The love ethic theory is only as good as the people who use it. hooks (1994) explains that the practitioner needs to work at making the theory effective in guiding actions that challenge lovelessness, violence and injustice. As long as ethical ideas are compatible with caring and anti-oppressive goals, they can be adapted and used. Thus, deontology theory and consequentialism can be used in a very selective manner in the love ethic approach with an extra level of caution regarding their assumptions and limitations. These tend to be the main theories that can collude with authoritarian regimes and laws or hide the social prevalence of harm, control and injustice. This is as much an issue about how power is used to disadvantage minority groups as the ideas per se. Citizens would want their government to be concerned about threats to national security (i.e., the greatest safety for the greatest number, consequentialism), but what constitutes a threat (where is the evidence of asylum seekers being a national threat in Australia?), and how it is responded to (treating them like prisoners and violating their human rights), need more than discriminatory legislation (deontology) or a consequentialist approach.

The revolutionary social worker stands with oppressed groups, links with other like-hearted people, and utilises the best of all the ethical theories in service of the public interest. A commitment is needed to ongoing learning, not so much of the formal ethical theories, as learning with and being changed by people, animals and nature without whom the revolution is not possible.

Synopsis of ethico-legal principles

Dear Reader,

I trust you found some of the ethical theories interesting, and as you can see there is such a richness of ideas to draw into a bundle that may work for you. As I said earlier, I am a cherry picker, one idea from this theory and another from that theory. You might prefer to adopt one main theory as your guide in practice. The aim is to ensure the bundling or theory is placed in an ethical sensibility which is anti-oppressive so you don't inadvertently become part of the oppression against others. The question 'Who is gaining in this situation, at whose expense?' can help determine what power dynamics are occurring. To be aware though, that this is a dualism which in itself can hide or oversimplify what Smith (1990) calls relations of ruling.

The paradox with all these ideas is that in practice we somehow need to place them just to one side of our awareness so we can meet with and engage the other individual - be they a person, animal or ecosystem - in an unencumbered way. I found in my first years as a practitioner I was so very earnest to 'do the right thing' - which is a good intention, as in good = ethical, right? Well ideas, assumptions, plans and solutions filling up your mind can get in the way of being present for, and listening to, the individual.

So be sure to leave room for the other individual to share their beliefs, interests and solutions as well.

We come now to the topic of ethico-legal principles. The intention of ethico-legal principles is to limit the authority of professionals and to protect the rights and interests of people seeking their services. Descriptions are provided of the traditional ethico-legal principles with the addition of some recommended new ones that are consistent with the love ethic. Relevant sources should be accessed before relying on the information provided here in practice. Professional codes of ethics and workplace policies and procedures are useful starting points for further details.

As you can see, I am very focused on putting this material together for you. I hope it is useful.

Duty of care

Duty of care refers to the care owed to service users by practitioners to: act in their best interests; avoid acting against the service user's interests; and, where inaction is the decision, this must also be in the service user's best interests. Duty of care involves "reasonable care [...] to avoid injury to another person or damage to property as a result of any action or inaction" (Johnson cited in Swain & Rice, 2009, p. 85).

The Australian Government's Department of Health describes duty of care as the practitioner's responsibility:

> [...] to their clients to reduce or limit the amount of harm or injury they may experience. This responsibility [...] can sometimes seem overwhelming. For example, our responsibility to one party (for example, our employer) might conflict deeply with our responsibility to our clients. It helps to remember that duty of care is a balancing act. (2004, n.p.)

They claim that there are several aspects to duty of care:

Legal - What does the law suggest we do?

Professional/ethical - What do other workers expect us to do?

Organisational - What does our organisation, and its funding body, say we should do?

Community - What do the [....] [families] of our clients and other community members expect us to do?

Personal - What do our own beliefs and values suggest we do?

We need to balance the safety of the [...] person against other concerns such as:

the safety of other people/our personal safety;

other rights of [...] people (e.g., the right to privacy);

the aims of the service (e.g., to empower [...] people); and,

the limits of our organisation (e.g., money and other resources). (Australian Government Department of Health, 2004, n.p.)

Some laws effectively put limits on an individual's duty of care restricting how they fulfil their duty in some way. This is because the legislation may override their common law duty of care if they are in conflict. For example, the Australian anti-discrimination laws require that the individual (in many situations) treat people equally regardless of, for example, their disability or mental illness, unless not discriminating would cause the individual unjustifiable cost or inconvenience. An example is where a restaurant owner would find their business is unviable if they were required to include wheelchair access to their facilities. This is discriminatory for the person in a wheelchair who wishes to dine at the restaurant but the case can be presented by the business owner nonetheless.

Love ethic informed guide for duty of care

Duty of care is of central importance in professional relationships. It is meant to ensure the individual's interests and wellbeing are upheld during their engagement with human services. Practitioners often have to grapple with the ethical tension of care and control where duty of care can involve actions against the individual's wishes or their best interests. This could be tempered by valuing a safeguarding approach which recognises the importance of affording the dignity of risk to the individual (Bamford, 2016) where they are actively supported to build self-empowerment and safety skills.

The politics of risk management is complex in the human services sector where legislation gives statutory authority for practitioners to act against an individual's self-determination. The principle of least restrictive practice, integral, for example, to mental health legislation (Queensland Government, 2017a) aims to limit this potentially coercive authority. Least restrictive practice means if it can be shown there is an option to maintain safety that is less coercive, this option needs to be used. The principle offers an ethical premise for proactively developing alternative ways of caring to the institutionalised and professionalised responses that currently predominate in the human services sector. Fostering non-coercive care options in mental health has been successful in community-based and holistic approaches which integrate medication with therapy, peer support, meaningful work and home-like spaces (see *Healing Homes*, Mackler, 2014a and *Open Dialogue*, Mackler, 2014b).

Duty to warn

This duty presumes a professional relationship exists where there is thereby a duty of care owed to the individual. At the same time there is a duty of care to absent individuals who may be subject to threats by that individual. If the practitioner perceives a threat to another individual, they are obliged to report threats of harm depending on the situation to the individual who is the target of the threat (McAuliffe, 2014, p. 124). This should be discussed with your supervisor and may involve the police.

In such circumstances, the practitioner would advise the individual making the threat they are enacting a duty to warn. This may also constitute grounds for breaking confidentiality. The duty to warn can indirectly protect the individual making the threats by ensuring the harm does not occur.

In summary, it is the idea that a practitioner who knew, or according to professional standards, should have known, that an individual posed a threat to another, has a duty to warn the intended victim.

Love ethic informed guide for duty to warn

The ethico-legal principle could be extended to include a duty to warn service users of the risks that may arise in accessing a service. This is the opposite to the tendency to judge service users who 'use the system' as if this is unethical. The iatrogenic effect in complex human service organisations draws attention to how systems can cause harm while professing to provide a service (see a mental health service user story, Waterhouse, 2014). Peer and Shabir (2018) describe this phenomenon as the health hazards that can accompany medical treatment. They argue that "most of the literature establishes that modern medicine is one of the major threats to world health" (Peer & Shabir,

2018, p. 309).

Informed consent

According to Wallace, this idea relates to consent, that is, permission given by the service user - whether to:

Disclose information to another person or agency, or

Be involved in particular therapy or to receive interventive techniques.

For that consent to be informed it needs to comprise three components:

That it is voluntary: i.e., not given under threat of duress or drugs and can be withdrawn, and

That information given must be specific to the act actually carried out, and

That they are judged to have competence or capacity - the individual must be an 'adult and of sound mind'. (1991, p. 57)

The issue of capacity is contested and in recognition of this, the Queensland Mental Health Act 2016 requires that capacity is assumed with some recognition that it can be fluctuating but cannot thereby be considered as an ongoing incapacity (Queensland Government, 2017b).

The AASW *Code of Ethics* explains informed consent in the following terms:

Social workers will ensure, as far as possible, that clients understand the principle of informed consent and the circumstances in which it may be required.

Where clients have limited capacity to comprehend or grant informed consent, social workers will provide information in accordance with the client's level of understanding and restrict their freedom of decision and action as little as possible. (2010, p. 27)

Love ethic informed guide for informed consent

Informed consent can provide the individual with considerable protection of their rights in situations where they are, for example, making

49

a decision to accept invasive treatment or to participate in research. The protection cannot, however, be assumed even if the practitioner has explained the circumstances of potential harm. Clarke's research with women who had experienced electro-convulsive treatment for mental health conditions found that the women felt they had no choice (Clarke, Barnes & Ross, 2018). While the womens' experiences were different, they came to believe from the doctor and other staff that this was their last chance to get relief from depression. This is in tension with the requirement for patients to freely provide informed consent for the treatment. It is a step that is required even if they are involuntary (unfree) under the mental health legislation.

The research questioned the medical bias which foreclosed other non-medical ways the women could be supported without the severe side effects of memory and identity loss. Clarke et al. (2018) recommend that mental health services need to engage in a more proactive and ongoing informed consent process with patients to address the coerciveness that can come with feeling desperate and having to take the medical advice no matter how inadequate the information about risks. Free, independent mental health legal advice has been shown to increase the complaints against mental health services. It can also challenge how the mental health legislation and related processes are being implemented (Mental Health Legal Centre, 2020).

Confidentiality

According to Bowles, Collingridge, Curry and Valentine, confidentiality refers to:

> The worker's obligation is not to disclose client information that is gained in the course of a professional relationship, or to use that information in a different context or for a different purpose, unless legally required or permitted to do so. Limits need to be clearly explained to client. Confidentiality meets obligations regarding respect for privacy and client self-determination. (2006, p. 155)

Confidentiality may need to be broken in certain circumstances such as:

Duty to warn another person of threat of harm

Court summons for information

Duty of care to the individual if they are at risk of harming themselves

Information that they have committed a crime

In situations of suspected child abuse.

The AASW explains that practitioners will only reveal confidential information in the circumstances outlined above provided it is permitted by law. The goal in most instances should be that "if by revealing information to relevant third parties an actual, identifiable risk of harm to a specific person or persons can be prevented" (AASW, 2010, p. 28).

Love ethic informed guide for confidentiality

Confidentiality is a highly valued ethico-legal principle in recognition of the legal right of the individual to privacy and control over information about themselves. Less recognised is how it can be used in ways that do not serve members of minority groups. For example, Australia's discriminatory policy of forcible removal of First Nation children from their families, known as the Stolen Generations (Bennett, 2019), was enabled by layers of secrecy and refusal to give families information about their children. Minajalku explains:

> With many Indigenous children enslaved in missions, reserves and children's homes, the practices were hidden from public scrutiny. In some institutions the names of children were changed and their origins were not recognised. (cited in Briskman, 2005, p. 213)

The social work profession was directly implicated in this attempt at genocide (Human Rights and Equal Opportunity Commission, 1997). The revolutionary social worker needs to be vigilant, especially with regard to legislation which is repressive, and seek ways to bring harm to individuals to the public's attention.

Procedural justice

Swain and Rice (2009) write that procedural justice, sometimes called natural justice, is concerned with the use of power and asks these questions:

What is the origin of the authority?

What are the limits of this authority?

Has it been validly exercised?

Further, procedural justice is about the duty to act fairly where the two guiding principles are the rule against bias and the right to a fair hearing (Swain & Rice, 2009, p. 87).

The American National Initiative for Building Community Trust and Justice (2020) is concerned with maintaining the public's support in policing work. The website describes procedural justice in the following way:

> Procedural justice is based on four central principles: treating people with dignity and respect, giving citizens 'voice' during encounters, being neutral in decision making, and conveying trustworthy motives.

> Research demonstrates that these principles contribute to relationships between authorities and the community in which: the community has trust and confidence in the police as honest, unbiased, benevolent, and lawful; the community feels obligated to follow the law and the dictates of legal authorities, and the community feels that it shares a common set of interests and values with the police. (American National Initiative for Building Community Trust and Justice, 2020, n.p.)

Love ethic informed guide for procedural justice

The Black Lives Matter (2020) movement arose from public concerns and outrage about black deaths when intercepted by the police in America. The National Initiative for Building Community Trust and Justice project is part of the criminal justice system's response to this public outcry.

Procedural justice is one of the main ways practitioners can enact social justice in the workplace, especially statutory workplaces governed by legislation where peoples' rights, status and entitlements can be adversely impacted. This can be where following the rules, if they are well formulated, transparent and fair, is recommended. It can serve as a protection against discrimination and minimise contextual influences such as targeting of revolutionary social workers for their activism on behalf of service users.

(Duty to Avoid) Negligence

Negligence is a term used in civil law (as distinct from criminal law). Claims of negligence need to be brought to a relevant court by aggrieved parties for compensation for harm caused. Negligence is based on the assumption that the practitioner owes the individual a duty of care. It assumes a professional relationship exists between the practitioner and service user and as such a duty of care exists.

Negligence refers to when a dereliction of duty of care has occurred. The service user has sustained damage as a result of the dereliction of duty. There is a direct relationship between the damage and the dereliction of duty of care, and a reasonable person could have been expected to foresee such damage occurring. The practitioner is expected to enact a duty to avoid negligence in their professional responsibilities toward the service user.

According to New South Wales state government's NSW *Civil Liability Act 2002*:

A person is not negligent in failing to take precautions against a risk of harm unless–

(a) the risk was foreseeable (that is, it is a risk of which the person knew or ought to have known), and

(b) the risk was not insignificant, and

(c) in the circumstances, a reasonable person in the person's position would have taken those precautions.

In determining whether a reasonable person would have taken precautions against a risk of harm, the court is to consider the following (amongst other relevant things)–

(a) the probability that the harm would occur if care were not taken,

(b) the likely seriousness of the harm,

(c) the burden of taking precautions to avoid the risk of harm,

(d) the social utility of the activity that creates the risk of harm.

The employer has ultimate responsibility for negligent acts on your part–

provided you are doing nothing that breaches acceptable standards, or doing anything that is considered criminal conduct.

In civil action, both the employee and the agency may be sued for negligence. (2002, 5B General Principles)

A failure of duty of care could result in a negligence claim.

Love ethic informed guide for duty to avoid negligence

The lived experience of an aggrieved individual may not be validated in a legal process. Further, their perception of negligence may not align with the legal definition. If you are the practitioner subject to negligence claims, it is an act of love and justice to ensure the aggrieved party has personal support and legal representation. Your ability to take responsibility for any harm done may be overtaken by employer strictures on your actions during the legal proceedings. Obtaining legal advice yourself is warranted, again with a critical understanding of what would be just for the aggrieved individual and your due accountability as the practitioner.

The idea of "therapeutic jurisprudence" or what Perlin calls "jurisprudence of healing" (cited in King, Freiberg, Batagol and Hyams, 2014, p. 20) is a developing area of non-adversarial legal practice that gives scope for love ethic informed accountability for harm done. In particular, the focus is on ensuring a "greater use of apology, forgiveness and reconciliation by judges and lawyers in their work (Dalcoff cited in King et al., 2014, p. 23).

Love ethic informed ethico-legal principles

In addition to the traditional ethico-legal principles, a love ethic informed approach suggests the accenting of the following ethical ideas. As such these recommended new ethico-legal principles should carry a moral weight and legal consequence.

Duty of non-maleficence

Non-maleficence needs to be recognised as embedded in all the ethico-legal principles as the baseline responsibility in professional practice. The American Psychological Association (2017) explains that this means not acting in ways that would unnecessarily or unjustifiably cause harm. Matters of unequal power, context and understandings of harm all have a bearing on the upholding this principle. A 'no harm' test could be designed to be decided by the individual or group in the least powerful position (Ross, 2017). This would extend legal notions of injury and harm to include moral injury (Bloom, 2017).

Duty of love of people, animals and nature

Love of people, animals and nature (Godden, 2017) needs to be recognised as already implicitly embedded in all the ethico-legal principles. Love of others is the ethical motivation to uphold these principles. The individuals who are engaged in professional situations can expect to feel they are treated with compassion, understanding, nonviolence and justice. High power individuals and groups can additionally expect to experience resistance, challenge and invitations to change behaviours which are experienced as harmful by others.

Duty of anti-discrimination

Anti-discrimination as an ethical premise implies that practitioners need to be accountable for any acts or omissions that cause or compound experiences of discrimination. This includes not participating in meta-discrimination with others in the workplace. Meta-discrimination (Sullivan, 1999) involves representing service users in negative or prejudicial ways, including in informal professional peer interactions. The duty also includes upholding all relevant anti-discrimination legislation and supporting workplaces that have obligations as part of occupational health and safety legislation. Duty of anti-discrimination recognises and upholds all international conventions and statements related to human rights and environmental sustainability. It implies the need for an international animals' rights convention.

Duty of ecojustice

A duty to uphold ecojustice is needed to extend social work's ethical regard to all beings as having intrinsic worth (Ross, 2020a). This duty includes social justice, species justice and environmental justice. Procedural justice processes are the building blocks for all types of justice work. Ideally, the advocates and representatives of animals and nature are given state protection and support similar to whistle-blowers who raise concerns in human service organisations.

The right to protest and gather in public places for nonviolent direct action also needs to be protected. It is the case, however, that collectivist rights to protest and strike are being restricted in some countries (Conde, 2017), including Australia (Smee, 2019). International research shows that resistance to development can result in protesters being assaulted or killed when trying to protect their homelands (Leahy, 2017).

Duty of environmental precautionary principle

The environmental precautionary principle is premised on caring for life and the natural world where the consequences of actions need to be considered. The Rio Declaration of 1992 explains that "where there are threats of serious or irreversible damage, lack of full scientific certainty shall not be used as a reason for postponing cost-effective measures to prevent environmental degradation" (UN Global Compact, 2020, n.p.).

It is typically included in environmental protection legislation, but this does not mean it is used. The duty to protect the environment can be upheld by a broad range of eco-activism and non co-operation with vested interests in the exploitation of nature. Eco-activism is where people power is focused on the strategic use of nonviolent direct action campaigns to challenge and change threats to environmental sustainability and diversity (Ross, Brueckner, Palmer & Eaglehawk, 2020).

Duty of social precautionary principle

The social precautionary principle extends this consideration of the fore-caring of life and the environment to risk and hazards that could impact people and communities. For example, Western Australia's *Public Health Act 2016* "places a legal duty on all people to conduct their activities in a way that does not cause harm to the health of others" (Western Australian Department of Health, 2016, para, 12).

Thus, the precautionary principle is implicit in public health legislation and needs to be embedded, strengthened and legally enforced in all legislation that impacts the rights and interests of people (see Ross, 2017). Public health and safety legislation can be subject to political pressure, for example, in the form of industry lobbying and their claims of scientific research showing there is no harm from their operations. Even where this is contested, it may not be sufficient to have the precautionary principle invoked (Ross & Puccio, 2020).

Duty of nonhuman animals precautionary principle

In relation to nonhuman animal species' survival and flourishing, this precautionary principle needs to be explicit in legislation that impacts the environment and the use and killing of animals for human consumption. It is weak in the absence of animal rights legislation, but there is some scope to embed it in, for example, *Victoria's Prevention of Cruelty to Animals Regulations 2019* (Principal Regulations) which extends animal protection provided under *Prevention of Cruelty to Animals Act 1986* (Victorian Government, 2020).

The idea of cruelty not being acceptable is integral to the legislation; however, the killing of some animals if it is done humanely is considered legal. Wild animals' rights have a chance to be protected under environmental protection legislation if the precautionary claim is upheld for their environment. Advocates for the lives of animals with economic value do not have recourse to the benefit of being able to argue the precautionary principle.

Anti-discrimination declarations, legislation and statements

Dear Reader,

Today a tree was cut down in my neighbourhood. It is very sad that this happened. We are surrounded by trees in my home town, in part because of the creeks that retain some rainforest remnants. One less tree will be noticed by the birds, insects and other animals who live nearby or who come to visit. Simard (2016) presents an inspiring video talk on how trees communicate with each other. Towards the end of the video she shows how her research using tracing elements implanted into trees reveals that the mother tree provides nutrients to her kin and also to different species of trees in her neighbourhood. The mother tree also sends warning signals when there is danger. The substances in these signals give an extra boost of protection to help the other trees survive. I hope it wasn't a mother tree who died today.

Did you find the ethico-legal principles and their respective challenges somewhat tempering of your revolutionary zeal? It can take some discernment to understand how to use which ones and when. They can be really useful if a critical understanding is fostered. Different practice situations can throw up different challenges. How perplexing is it that there can be a risk in enacting a duty of care where we may be acting against what the person wants? Are we thereby being controlling when we are trying to help? This is one of the most troubling experiences for a practitioner as it goes against our professional values.

I can remember every time a person in a service user role has protested to me that my actions were against their wishes, and that they felt variations on the theme of betrayal. It is for this reason that I am not a purest deontologist. I have acted to uphold statutory or agency obligations against the service user more times than I really want to remember. I justified it at the time, but now in hindsight I can't justify my actions quite so suredly.

I've added to the conventional ethico-legal principles to increase the ethical language and action options for revolutionary practice. These have helped me in recent times and situations.

I have become much more attuned to international declarations and anti-discriminatory legislation. This has resulted in me enabling a person to be aware of their legal rights in situations of coercion. It is for this reason that I thought a section outlining some of these documents and laws might be useful for you to have in one place.

It is important to have up-to-date knowledge of the range of declarations of rights, conventions, legislation and public statements that support anti-discrimination and doing no harm. These documents embed ethics and, in the case of legislation, a degree of legal authority that can be appealed to as part of upholding the public interest. The material provided is illustrative not exhaustive and predominantly draws on Australian legislation to show the relevant material that can be sourced.

Human rights

The United Nations website, particularly the Human Rights Office of the High Commissioner, provides an extensive resource of international conventions, bodies and statements, for example:

The Universal Declaration of Human Rights

Source: http://www.un.org/en/universal-declaration-human-rights/.

Also see:

https://www.ohchr.org/EN/ProfessionalInterest/Pages/UniversalHumanRightsInstruments.aspx

Including:

Convention on the Rights of Children

Convention on the Rights of Persons with Disabilities

Convention on the Prevention and Punishment of the Crime of Genocide

Declaration on the Rights of Indigenous Peoples

Declaration on the Protection of All Persons from Being Subjected to Torture and Other Cruel, Inhuman, or Degrading Treatment or Punishment

Freedom of Association and Protection of the Right to Organise Convention, 1948 (No. 87)

International Covenant on Economic, Social and Cultural Rights 1966

International Covenant on Civil and Political Rights 1966

Note: There is no declaration on the rights of animals or the planet.

The Australian Human Rights Commission has statutory responsibilities under:

Age Discrimination Act 2004

Disability Discrimination Act 1992

Racial Discrimination Act 1975

Sex Discrimination Act 1984

Fair Work Act 2009

And see relevant state anti-discrimination acts. For example:

Anti-Discrimination Act 1991 (QLD)

Source: https://www.humanrights.gov.au/our-work/employers/quick-guide-australian-discrimination-laws

Human Rights Act 2019 (Queensland)

See: https://www.qai.org.au/2019/06/06/factsheet-human-rights-act-2019-qld/

Occupational health and safety legislation

Employers in Australia have a legal responsibility to ensure safe work-places. For example, *Victoria's Occupational Health and Safety Act 2004* (and see other relevant acts on this link)

Source: https://www.ohsrep.org.au/overview_of_ohs_and_related_legislation

Human service organisations typically have policies which reflect anti-discrimination legislation and include anti-harassment and anti-bullying policies.

Minority groups' activism causing legislative change

Public activism against injustice plays an important role in challenging unfair legislation. For example, the public pressure to make marriage legal between same sex couples in Australia:

Marriage Amendment (Definition and Religious Freedoms) Act 2017

Source: https://www.legislation.gov.au/Details/C2017A00129

Australian First Nation Peoples' struggles for sovereignty and land claims have involved ongoing resistance, campaigns and lobbying of the power elites. There have been a small number of occasions where this activism has translated into legislation. For example, the High Court decision to recognise the prior occupation of Australia by Aboriginal and Torres Strait Islander People at the time of white settlement resulted in:

Native Title Act 1993

Source: https://aiatsis.gov.au/explore/articles/land-rights

However, this legislation in a context of systemic racism and mining industry political influence has not resulted in the upholding of exclusive rights of First Nation communities, even if they can show ongoing connection with the land. Mining companies are typically given rights to operate, with local communities offered compensation (Woodley, 2020). The compensation is not commensurate with the royalties paid to the government or the profit to be retained by the mining company

(Cleary, 2017).

An historically significant gathering of First Nation People in 2017 resulted in a call for the Australian Government to work with them to recognise First Nation People in the constitution and to form an arm of government where they can represent the interests of First Nation People:

Uluru Statement from the Heart (2017) [Referendum Council]

Source: https://www.referendumcouncil.org.au/sites/default/files/2017-05/Uluru_Statement_From_The_Heart_0.PDF

And: https://ulurustatement.org/our-story

When the prime minister was presented with the statement, without any public conversation, he said no.

The state government of Victoria is the first state to move towards the recognition of First Nation Peoples' right to be recognised (see Dunstan, 2019):

Victorian Treaty with Aboriginal People

Source: https://www.aboriginalvictoria.vic.gov.au/treaty

This has yet to be legislated.

International statements on sustainable development, the environment and human wellbeing

UN Millennium Development Goals

Source: https://www.un.org/millenniumgoals/

United Nations Climate Change Kyoto Protocol 2005, which operationalises the United Nations Framework Convention on Climate Change

Source: https://unfccc.int/kyoto_protocol

UN Sustainable Development Goals

Source: https://sustainabledevelopment.un.org/?menu=1300

Laws affecting the environment

The Queensland law handbook has useful resources in relation to the environment:

The Environment Protection and Biodiversity Conservation Act

Environmental harm

Environmental pollution

Climate change

Cultural heritage

Taking action to protect the environment

Support for taking action to protect the environment.

Specifically, the *Environmental Protection Act 1994*, and the environmental precautionary principle (see earlier segment and Martuzzi & Tickner, 2004).

Source: https://queenslandlawhandbook.org.au/the-queensland-law-handbook/living-and-working-in-society/laws-affecting-the-environment/

Animal rights organisations

Some of the key pro-animal rights groups are:

People for the Ethical Treatment of Animals PETA (2020) *Animals are not ours.*

Source: https://www.peta.org/

The Nonhuman Rights Project

Source: https://www.nonhumanrights.org/

Voiceless, The Animal Protection Institute

Source: https://www.voiceless.org.au/

Also see Petrsak (2018) on the need for nonhuman animals and nature to be included in the Universal Declaration of Human Rights.

Love ethic informed guide

The inclusion of material in this section means each piece needs to be interrogated for any limitations in its professed anti-discriminatory rationale and goals. Further, the challenge with anti-discriminatory declarations and legislation is ensuring they are upheld. The United Nations (UN) Human Rights Office of the High Commissioner provides human rights experts - special rapporteurs - who can be called upon to investigate human rights abuses. The responsibilities of the experts are outlined in *Special Procedures of the Human Rights Council* and they report to the UN General Assembly (UN, 2020). The issue of intimidation and reprisal against individuals and groups who support this work is recognised as a growing problem. The UN special rapporteurs visited Australia to investigate reports of human rights abuses against asylum seekers detained in offshore prison-like centres. The Australian Government effectively told them to mind their business and to not interfere in Australia's sovereign interests (Doherty, 2017).

Legislation such as state governments' mental health, domestic violence and child safety acts are not included in this selection. The legislation requires a developed analysis before it can be included, if at all, in a synopsis of anti-discriminatory legislation, albeit for different reasons. For example, in relation to mental health legislation in Australia, there are strenuous efforts to protect the interests of the individual. However, no other area of health care involves forced treatment against a non-consenting individual. The research shows that some types of treatment such as seclusion cause trauma and may constitute torture and the abuse of the individual's human rights (Ross, 2018).

It remains important for the practitioner to be well informed about the relevant legislation and other public statements to maintain a critical understanding of the discriminatory and coercive aspects alongside a reflexive stance in your own practice.

Conclusion

Dear Reader,

Well, what did you think? You can let me know by writing to the publisher.

You most likely have other ideas and resources you can add to the last section that you have found helpful. Knowing where the closest legal aid centre is would be one good bit of information to have at your fingertips. Knowing someone at that legal aid centre who you can get advice from and recommend to service users would be the next best thing. Sometimes important resources can be in your workplace. For example, in the state mental health services there is a person, often in an administration role, who manages all the paperwork related to the Mental Health Act. It has never ceased to amaze me how knowledgeable they are about what is possible and what is needed in specific situations, including ideas for maximising the patient's rights. So seek out such people and make them your professional friend.

That's all from me for now.

The cooler autumn air is so welcome after a long dry and then really wet summer.

We are working flat out at the university where I teach to place our courses online to protect staff and students from the coronavirus outbreak.

Wherever you are I hope you have kept well and that your family and community are also safe.

Dyann

May, 2020

Further reading

Any introductory text for social work and the helping professions typically have a useful summary of ethics and ethical theories, for example:

Chenoweth, L., & McAuliffe, D. (2017). Locating the lighthouse: Values & ethics in practice, in *The road to social work and human service practice* (4th edn.). Cengage Learning. Chapter 3, pp. 59-91.

Morley, C., Macfarlane, S., & Ablett, P. (2019). Values and ethics for critical practice, in *Engaging with social work: A critical introduction* (2nd edn.). Cambridge. Chapter 5, pp. 107-133.

In the broader helping professions, a key text is:

Corey, G., Schneider Corey, M., & Corey, C. (2019). *Issues and ethics in the helping professions* (10th edn.). Brookes/Cole Cengage Learning.

There are a number of social work texts dedicated to values and ethics, for example:

Banks, S. (2012). *Ethics and values in social work*. Palgrave Macmillan.

Barsky, A. (2019). *Ethics and values in social work* (2nd edn.). Oxford University Press.

Beckett, C., Maynard, A., & Jordan, P. (2017). *Values and ethics in social work* (3rd edn.). Sage.

Clifford, D., & Bourke, B. (2009). *Anti-oppressive ethics and values in social work*. Palgrave Macmillan.

Hugman R. (2013). *Culture, values & ethics in social work*. Routledge.

Pease, B., Vreugdenhil, A., & Stanford, S. (Eds.). (2018). *Critical ethics of care in social work: Transforming the politics and practices of caring*. Routledge.

Pullen-Sansfacon, A., & Cowden, S. (2012). *The ethical foundations of social work*. Pearson.

References

American Psychological Association (2017). *Ethical principles of psychologists and code of conduct.* https://www.apa.org/ethics/code/ethics-code-2017.pdf

Australian Association of Social Workers (AASW) (2010). *Code of ethics.* AASW.

Australian Government Department of Health (2004). *Duty of care issues.* https://www1.health.gov.au/internet/publications/publishing.nsf/Content/drugtreat-pubs-front11-wk-toc~drug-treat-pubs-front11-wk-secb~drugtreat-pubs-front11-wk-secb-6~drugtreat-pubs-front11-wk-secb-6-1

Bamford, W. (2016). *Duty of care and the dignity of risk.* https://interchangewa.org.au/opinion/duty-care-dignity-risk/

Banks, S. (2012). *Ethics and values in social work* (4th ed.). Palgrave Macmillan.

Banks, S. (2016). Everyday ethics in professional life: Social work as ethics work. *Ethics and Social Welfare, 10*(1), 35-52.

Banks, S., & Gallagher, A. (2009). *Ethics in professional life: Virtues for health and social care.* Palgrave Macmillan.

Barnes, G. , & Newhouse, G. (2015). *Border Force Act: Detention secrecy just got worse.* https://www.abc.net.au/news/2015-05-28/barns-newhouse-detention-centre-secrecy-just-got-even-worse/6501086

Beckett, C., Maynard, A., & Jordan, P. (2017). *Values and ethics in social work* (3rd ed.). Sage.

Bennett, B. (2019). The importance of Aboriginal history for practitioners. In B. Bennett & S. Green (Eds.), *Our voices: Aboriginal social work* (pp. 3-30). Red Globe Press.

Bettcher, T. (2015). *Intersexuality, transgender and transsexuality.* https://www.oxfordhandbooks.com/view/10.1093/oxfordhb/9780199328581.001.0001/oxford-hb-9780199328581-e-21

Black Lives Matter (2020). *September 2018: Stephon Clark.* https://blacklivesmatter.com/global-actions/

Bloom, S. (2017). *The sanctuary model: Through the lens of moral safety.* http://www.sanctuaryweb.com/Portals/0/Bloom%20Pubs/2017%20Bloom%20Sanctuary%20Moral%20APA%20Handbook.pdf

Boetto, H. (2019). Advancing transformative eco-social change: Shifting from modernist to holistic foundations. *Australian Social Work, 72*(2), 139–151.

Bolton, R. (1986). *People skills.* Simon & Schuster.

Braidotti, R. (2013). *The posthuman.* Polity Press.

Braidotti, R. (2018). A theoretical framework for the critical posthumanities. *Theory, Culture and Society, 0*(0), 1-13.

Bowles, W., Collingridge, M., Curry, S., & Valentine, B. (2006). *Ethical practice in social work: An applied approach.* Allen & Unwin.

Briskman, L. (2005). Reclaiming humanity for asylum seekers: A social work response. *International Social Work, 48*(6), 714-724.

Baltra-Ulloa, A. (2018). Speaking of care from the periphery: The politics of caring from the postcolonial margins. In Pease, B., Vreugdenhil, A., & Stanford, S. (Eds.), *Critical ethics of care in social work: Transforming the politics and practices of caring* (pp. 129-138). Routledge.

Buber, M. (1970). *I and Thou.* (trans. W. Kaufmann). Simon & Schuster.

Butler, J. (1990). *Gender trouble: Feminism and the subversion of identity.* Routledge.

Chopra, D. (1997). *The path to love.* Rider.

Clark, K., Barnes, M., & Ross, D. (2018). 'I had no other option': Women, ECT and informed consent. *Journal of Mental Health Nursing, 27,* 1077-1085.

Cleary, P. (2017). *Title fight: The great philanthropist vs the people of the Pilbara.* https://www.themonthly.com.au/issue/2017/september/1504188000/paul-cleary/title-fight

Clifford, D., & Bourke, B. (2009). *Anti-oppressive ethics and values in social work.* Palgrave Macmillan.

Conde, M. (2017). Resistance to mining: A review. *Ecological Economics, 132,* 80-90.

Doherty, B. (2016). *Doctors are freed to speak about Australia's detention regime after U-turn.* https://www.theguardian.com/australia-news/2016/oct/20/doctors-freed-to-speak-about-australias-detention-regime-after-u-turn

Doherty, B. (2017). *UN official says Australia responsible for 'inhuman' treatment of asylum seekers.* https://www.theguardian.com/australia-news/2017/jun/12/un-official-says-australia-responsible-for-inhuman-treatment-of-asylum-seekers

Doyle, S. (2016). *Trainwreck: The women we love to hate, mock and fear ... and why.* Melville House.

Doyle, S. (2019). *Dead blondes and bad mothers.* Penguin Books.

Dunstan, J. (2019). *Victorian Aboriginal voters have elected an Assembly to advance the treaty process. So what's next?* https://www.abc.net.au/news/2019-11-05/victorian-aboriginal-treaty-assembly-elected-what-happens-next/11650520

Fook, J. (2016). *Social work: A critical approach to practice.* Sage.

Fisher-Borne, M., Montana Cain, J., & Martin, S. (2015). From mastery to accountability: Cultural humility as an alternative to cultural competence. *Social Work Education, 34*(2), 165-181.

Francione, G., & Charlton, A. (2013). *Animal rights: The abolitionist approach.* Exempla Press.

Fraser, N. (2009). Who counts? Dilemmas of justice in a post westphalian world. *Antipode, 41*(1), 281-297.

Freire, P. (1970). *Pedagogy of the oppressed*. Penguin Books.

Funston, L. (2013). Aboriginal and Torres Strait Islander worldviews and cultural safety transforming sexual assault service provision for children and young people. *International Journal of Environmental Research Public Health, 10*(9), 3818-3833.

Fuss, D. (Ed.). (1991). *Inside/out: Lesbian theories, gay theories*. Routledge.

Godden, N. (2017). The love ethic: A radical theory for social work practice. *Australian Social Work, 70*(4), 405-416.

Green, S. (2018). Aboriginal people and caring within a colonised society. In B. Pease, A. Vreugdenhil & S. Stanford (Eds.). *Critical ethics of care in social work: Transforming the politics and practices of caring* (pp. 139-147). Routledge.

Happell, B., & Scholz, B. (2017). Doing what we can, but knowing our place: Being an ally to promote consumer leadership in mental health. *International Journal of Mental Health Nursing, 27*(1), 440-447.

Haraway, D. (2006). A cyborg manifesto: Science, technology and socialist feminism in the late twentieth century. In J. Weiss, J. Nolan, J. Hunsinger, & P. Trifonas (Eds.). *The international handbook of virtual learning environments* (pp. 117-158). Springer.

Haraway, D. (2010). *When species meet*. University of Minnesota.

Haraway, D. (2017). *Staying with the trouble: Making kin in the Chthulucene*. Duke University Press.

Hill Collins, P. (1990). *Black feminist thought: Knowledge, consciousness and the politics of empowerment*. Harper Collins.

hooks, b. (1994). *Outlaw culture: Resisting representations*. Routledge.

hooks, b. (2000). *Feminism is for everybody*. Pluto Press.

hooks, b. (2001). *Salvation: Black people and love*. William Morrow.

Hughes, M. (2018). Where is the love? Meditations on a critical ethic of care and love in social work. In B. Pease, A. Vreugdenhil & S. Stanford (Eds.), *Critical ethics of care in social work: Transforming the politics and practices of caring* (pp. 197-206). Routledge.

Hugman, R. (2013). *Culture, values & ethics in social work*. Routledge.

Human Rights and Equal Opportunity Commission (1997). *Bringing them home. Report of the national inquiry into the separation of Aboriginal and Torres Strait Islander children from their families.* https://www.humanrights.gov.au/sites/default/files/content/pdf/social_justice/bringing_them_home_report.pdf

King, M., Freiberg, A., Batagol, B., & Hyams, R. (2014). *Non-adversarial justice*. The Federation Press.

Leahy, S. (2017). *200 environmentalists were murdered last year.* https://www.nationalgeographic.com/news/2017/07/environmental-ists-protestors-killed-violence-global-witness-report/

Lennard, N., & Wolfe, C. (2017). *Is humanism really humane?* https://www.nytimes.com/2017/01/09/opinion/is-humanism-really-hu-mane.html

Mackler, D. (2014a). *Healing homes: Recovery from psychosis without medication.* https://youtu.be/JV4NTEp8S2Q

Mackler, D. (2014b). *Open dialogue: An alternative Finnish approach to healing psychosis.* https://youtu.be/HDVhZHJagfQ

Martuzzi, M., & Tickner, J. (Eds.). (2004). *The precautionary principle: Protecting public health, the environment and the future of our children.* http://www.euro.who.int/__data/assets/pdf_file/0003/91173/E83079.pdf

McAuliffe, D. (2014). *Interprofessional ethics: Collaboration in the social, health & human services.* Cambridge University Press.

McDonald, F., & Then, S. (2014). *Ethics, law & healthcare: A guide for nurses and midwives.* Palgrave Macmillan.

Mental Health Legal Centre (2020). *Our vision, purpose and values.* https://mhlc.org.au/about-us/vision-purpose-and-values/

Miehls, D., & Moffatt, K. (2000). Constructing social work identity based on the reflective self. *British Journal of Social Work, 30*(3), 339-348.

Mullaly, B., & West, J. (2017). *Challenging oppression & confronting privilege* (3rd ed.). Oxford University Press.

National Initiative for Building Community Trust and Justice (2020).

Procedural justice. https://trustandjustice.org/resources/intervention/procedural-justice

New South Wales Government (2002). *Civil Liability Act 2002 – Sect 5B*. http://www5.austlii.edu.au/au/legis/nsw/consol_act/cla2002161/s5b.html

Nhat Hahn, T. (1996). *Cultivating the mind of love*. Paralax Press.

Nhat Hahn, T. (2001). *Anger: Wisdom for cooling the flames*. Riverhead Books.

Oscar, J., & Little, R. (2019). *Our choices, our voices: Close the gap*. https://www.humanrights.gov.au/our-work/aboriginal-and-torres-strait-islander-social-justice/publications/close-gap-report-our

Pease, B., Vreugdenhil, A., & Stanford, S. (Eds.). (2018). *Critical ethics of care in social work: Transforming the politics and practices of caring*. Routledge.

Peer, R., & Shabi, N. (2018). Iatrogenesis: A review on nature, extent and distribution of healthcare hazards. *Journal of Family Medical and Primary Care, 7*(2), 309-314.

Petrsak, D. (2018). *Human and non-human rights – convergence or conflict?* https://www.openglobalrights.org/human-and-non-human-rights-convergence-or-conflict/

Plumwood, V. (1993). *Feminism and the mastery of nature*. Routledge.

Plumwood, V. (2000). Integrating ethical framework for animals, humans and nature: A critical feminist ecological-societal analysis. *Ethics and the Environment, 5*(2), 285-322.

Plumwood, V. (2002). *Environmental culture: The ecological crisis of reason*. Routledge.

Poelina, A. (2020). Foreward. First Law is the natural law of the land. In D. Ross, M. Brueckner, M. Palmer & W. Eaglehawk (Eds.), *Eco-activism & social work: New directions in leadership and group work* (pp. viii-xii). Routledge.

Pullen-Sansfacon, A., & Cowden, S. (2012). *The ethical foundations of social work*. Pearson.

Queensland Government (2009). *Right to Information Act 2009.*

https://www.oic.qld.gov.au/guidelines/for-government/access-and-amendment/decision-making/public-interest-balancing-test

Queensland Government (2017a). *Mental Health Act 2016: Fact Sheets – Objects and Principles*. Queensland Government.

Queensland Government (2017b). *Chief psychiatrist policy*. https://www.health.qld.gov.au/__data/assets/pdf_file/0018/465210/cpp-treatment-criteria-capacity.pdf

Rawls, J. (1971). *A theory of justice*. Oxford University Press.

Rogers, C. (1951/2003). *Client-centred therapy*. Little, Brown Book Group.

Rosenberg, M. (2009). *Four part nonviolent communication (NVC) process*. https://www.nonviolentcommunication.com/pdf_files/4part_nvc_process.pdf

Ross, D. (2017). A research-based model for corporate social responsibility: Towards accountability to impacted stakeholders. *Journal of Corporate Social Responsibility, 2*(8), 1-11.

Ross, D. (2018). A social work perspective on seclusion and restraint in Australia's public mental health system. *Journal of Progressive Human Services: Radical Thought and Praxis, 29*(1), 1-19.

Ross, D. (2020a). The love ethic practice model. In D. Ross, M. Brueckner, M. Palmer & W. Eaglehawk (Eds.), *Eco-activism & social work: New directions in leadership and group work* (pp. 125-142). Routledge.

Ross, D. (2020b). Ethic of love. In S. Idowu, & R. Schmidpeter, N. Capaldi, L. Zu, M. Del Baldo & R. Abreu (Eds.), *International encyclopedia of sustainable management*. Springer Reference. [In press].

Ross, D., Brueckner, M., Palmer, M., & Eaglehawk, W. (Eds.). (2020). *Eco-activism & social work: New directions in leadership and group work*. Routledge.

Ross, D., & Palmer, M. (2020). Transformational change leadership and dialogue between groups. In D. Ross, M. Brueckner, M. Palmer & W. Eaglehawk (Eds.), *Eco-activism & social work: New directions in leadership and group work* (pp. 143-162). Routledge.

Ross, D., & Puccio, V. (2020). Homegrown community activism in Yarloop. In D. Ross, M. Brueckner, M. Palmer & W. Eaglehawk (Eds.), *Eco-activism & social work: New directions in leadership and group work* (pp. 26-38). Routledge.

Ryan, T. (2011). *Animals and social work: A moral introduction.* Palgrave Macmillan.

Saleebey, D. (2012). *The strengths perspective in social work practice* (6th ed.). Pearson.

Shiva, V., & Mies, M. (2014). *Ecofeminism: Critique, influence, change.* Zed Books.

Simard, S. (2016). *How trees talk to each other.* https://www.youtube.com/watch?v=Un2yBgIAxYs

Singer, P. (2015). *Nonhuman animal ethics.* https://youtu.be/TgRoZVT-6kYc

Smee, B. (2019). *Queensland anti-protest laws 'inherently disproportionate', UN human rights experts say.* https://www.theguardian.com/australia-news/2019/dec/13/queensland-anti-protest-laws-inherently-disproportionate-un-human-rights-experts-say

Smith, D. (1990). *The conceptual practices of power: A feminist sociology of knowledge.* Northeastern University Press.

Smith, L. (1999). *Decolonizing methodologies: Research and Indigenous peoples.* Zed Books Ltd.

Stanley, L., & Wise, S. (1993). *Breaking out again: Feminist ontology and epistemology.* Routledge.

Sullivan, E. (1999). Discrimination and 'meta-discrimination': Issues for reflective practice. *Australian Social Work, 52*(3), 3-8.

Swain, P., & Rice, R. (Eds.). *In the shadow of the law: The legal context of social work practice* (3rd ed.). The Federation Press.

The Dalai Lama (1997). *The joy of living and dying in peace.* Harper Collins Publishers.

Tong, R. (1998). The ethics of care: a feminist virtue ethics of care for health practitioners. *Journal of Medicine & Philosophy, 23*(2), 113-152.

Tzu, L. (4th Century BC). *Tao de ching.* https://www.taoistic.com/tao-themes/

UN Human Rights Office of the High Commissioner (2020). *Special procedures of the Human Rights Council.* https://www.ohchr.org/en/hrbodies/sp/pages/welcomepage.aspx

UN Global Compact (2020). *Principle 7: Environment.* https://www.unglobalcompact.org/what-is-gc/mission/principles/principle-7

Van Stichel, E. (2014). Love and justice's dialectical relationship. *Medical Health Care & Philosophy, 17,* 499-508.

Victorian Government (2020). *Prevention of cruelty to animals legislation.* http://agriculture.vic.gov.au/agriculture/animal-health-and-welfare/animal-welfare/animal-welfare-legislation/prevention-of-cruelty-to-animals-legislation

Wallace, M. (1991). *Health care and the law.* The Law Book Company.

Waterhouse, B. (2014). I'm not mad! *Social Alternatives, 33*(3), 15-19.

Watson, L. (1988). An Aboriginal perspective: Developing an Indigenous social work. In E. Chamberlain (Ed.), *Change and continuity in Australian social work* (pp. 177- 184). Longman.

West, C. (2011). *Cornell West: Justice is what love looks like in public.* https://www.youtube.com/watch?v=nGqP7S_WO6o.

Western Australian Government (2016). *Western Australia's Public Health Act of 2016.* https://www.legislation.wa.gov.au/legislation/statutes.nsf/law_a147114.html

White, R. (2018). Ecocentrism & criminal justice. *Theoretical Criminology, 22*(3), 342-362.

Woodley, M. (2020). The wrong side of Native title, the right side of mining. In D. Ross, M. Brueckner, M. Palmer and W. Eaglehawk (Eds.), *Eco-activism and social work. New directions in leadership and group work* (pp. 61-73). Routledge.

www.ingramcontent.com/pod-product-compliance
Lightning Source LLC
Chambersburg PA
CBHW032153020426
42334CB00016B/1274